How to Read With Your Children

Educator/Workshop Leader's Guide

by Phyllis A. Wilken

Edited by Jami McCormick
Text layout/design and cover by Sherri Rowe
Illustrated by Terry Rowe

ISBN #1-57035-114-7

Printed in the United States of America

Published and Distributed by:

Sopris West
1140 Boston Avenue • Longmont, CO 80501 • (303) 651-2829
http://www.sopriswest.com

Dedication

I dedicate this guide to family reading and to my family which spans four generations. This family photo represents three generations. We all enjoy reading together and individually and have great, long discussions about what we have read.

The four women in the photo have a combined total of 75 years of teaching experience. Lyndell has taught grades 1-12, and is

Royce Wilken, Delmar Wilken, Lyndell Wilken, Kent Hunter
Tyler Wilken, Lois Wilken, Phyllis Wilken, Mylla Wilken Hunter, Zachary Wilken

presently teaching at Lane Community College in Eugene, Oregon. Lois taught grades 1-6 in Nebraska, near Omaha. She is now a stay-at-home parent and volunteers many hours in Ellisville Elementary and Crestwood Middle School in Missouri, is a Scout Leader, and is a church and Vacation Bible School teacher and coordinator. Mylla taught first grade in Houston, Texas and third grade at Palos Park, Illinois. She has been an assistant principal there, and is presently serving as the coordinator of the district's Emergent Literacy Program.

The men are avid readers too! Royce works for Archer Daniels Midland (ADM) in St. Louis, Kent is a self-employed communications consultant, and my husband is professor emeritus of agricultural economics at the University of Illinois. Thanks to him for putting this guide on the word processor.

Our two grandsons, Tyler and Zachary, love reading! When they visit it is my great privilege to read special books to them—the books I read to our children! Those books are their favorites and they still occupy a special place in our house and always will.

My mother, Kathryn Anderson, is not pictured here. But I owe my creativity and my love for reading to her. As a mother of seven children, she did not have much time for reading to us. However, Sunday evenings were devoted to family activities led by my mother. She would draw cartoons and together we would make up appropriate stories for them. That activity was followed by reading a Bible story and then another story. It was a time of learning about my mother's values and beliefs, and my brothers' and sisters' interests and opinions. It was a special time in my life. So my family reading experiences span four generations! I wish all children had that kind of mother.

this guide is also dedicated to all parents and caregivers who will be motivated to read with their children because they read this guide. If you have not started reading with your children or grandchildren, do so now. Remember, you are your children's first, favorite, and most influential teacher. You are not only reading to and for them, but also their children and their grandchildren. Love of reading and the value derived from it carries over from generation to generation.

Acknowledgments

I wish to thank the following people: Dr. Carolyn Farrar, manager, and Robert Rush, principal consultant of the Intervention and Improvement section of Chapter 1, Illinois State Board of Education, who funded the project "What To Do When You Read With Children," which provided the content for this guide; Jane Quinlan, Illinois Regional Office of Education, who administered the grant; Jean Osborn, associate director of the Center for the Study of Reading, who directed this study and encouraged me to write this guide; Dr. Judith Barbour who wrote the literature review and analysis; Terry Denny, professor emeritus, Educational Psychology, University of Illinois, who was an expert in the interpretation and analysis of the results; and the 241 people who completed the questionnaires.

About the Author

Phyllis A. Wilken began her 50-year career as an educator in a one-room school house in Cullom, Illinois teaching grades 1-8. She became a curriculum coordinator, then an acting middle school assistant principal before becoming the principal at Garden Hills Elementary School in Champaign, Illinois. Her own experiences first as a teacher, then as a parent, and finally as an administrator showed her the importance of paying attention to individual children's needs. She guided Garden Hills on an improvement mission that resulted in the school receiving the United States Department of Education's Blue Ribbon Award for Excellence in Elementary Education.

From 1945, in a Cullom, Illinois one-room rural school to Champaign, Illinois Garden Hills Elementary School's Blue Ribbon Award for Excellence, Phyllis A. Wilken shares her experience and enthusiasm for creating excellence in education by involving parents/caregivers and making them partners in their children's learning.

Phyllis Wilken and the staff involved parents in their children's learning by developing a family reading program, helping them with homework, and encouraging them to attend school activities. She involved parents in their children's schooling by promoting communication, cooperation, and collaboration among the school staff and parents to maximize the learning of the students.

Since her retirement in 1987 she has served as a educational consultant for the University of Illinois, College of Education, Center for the Study of Reading. She worked with E.D. Hirsch, author of *Cultural Literacy*, on the development of the six books *What Your 1st-6th Grader Needs to Know* and *A First Dictionary of Cultural Literacy*. She has served on many boards and committees, including, from 1990-1994, the U.S. Office of Education review panel that selected the National Diffusion Network model reading programs and the Blue Ribbon Elementary Schools, as well as the Illinois State Board of Education Retired Administrative Services Committee. She received the National Association of Direct Instruction Award for Administrators, the Outstanding Educator Award conferred by the YWCA, and the Illinois Regional Office of Education Award. She is listed in

Who's Who of American Women and *Outstanding Elementary Teachers in America*. She currently is the president of the University of Illinois College of Education Alumni Board, and has received the University of Illinois College of Education Outstanding Alumni Award.

She is also the author of a book about Garden Hills Elementary School's journey to excellence entitled *Turning Our School Around: Seven Commonsense Steps to School Improvement*.

Table of Contents

Section One

Introduction to the Program

Why Educators Should Facilitate Family Reading

All educators would agree that reading is a skill critical to lifelong learning. Different educators, however, will have varying beliefs about the best way to teach children to read. Whether a proponent of "skills-based" or "whole language" instruction, this simple program will help you to encourage the parents of your preschool or primary grade students to read with their children on a regular basis.

Why facilitate such family reading? Because today more than ever many students are not learning to read proficiently, and this is due in part to a lack of language development and reading to preschoolers in their homes or daycare facilities. The following appeared in *USA Today* (Kelly & Hellmich, 1996), and a vast body of research shows that family reading with young children promotes reading readiness and is a key to later success in reading at school.

Many Parents Don't Read to Their Children

Experts highly recommend reading to kids frequently. But only 39% of parents with children under three read or look at picture books with their little ones at least once a day, says a new poll of 2,017 parents with kids this age. And 16% of parents do not read to their young kids at all.

Although book-sharing activities are higher for toddlers than infants, rates are still low. Only 48% of parents with kids ages one to three years read to or show a picture book to their child at least once a day.

The poll was conducted for the Commonwealth Fund, a New York-based nonprofit foundation that studies health and social issues. The survey has a margin of error of three percentage points.

As long ago as 1908, E.B. Huey, in *The Psychology and Pedagogy of Reading*, made the statement: "The secret of it all lies in the parents' reading aloud to and with the child" (p. 332). This statement could easily be said to reflect today's thinking about the value of parents/caregivers reading aloud to their children. Many educators and researchers feel that there is a positive relationship between being read to at home and various aspects of oral and written language development in children at school (Chomsky, 1972; Durkin, 1966; Harkness, 1981). Almost every reading methods textbook and early childhood education textbook, plus numerous articles, recommend that parents/caregivers read to their young children in order to prepare them well for the learning that will take place in school. Supporting these beliefs in the past century are many studies that have shown that reading to children can be a very important part of their becoming literate and developing a positive attitude toward reading that will be carried throughout life.

One of the earliest studies of young readers was done by Durkin (1966). Her findings are relevant:

> *First, in doing the research itself, it became clear that early readers are not a special brand of children who can be readily identified and sorted by tests. Rather, it would seem, it is their mothers who play the key role in effecting the early achievement. The homes they provide, the example they show, the time they give to the children, their concepts of their role as educator of the preschool child—all of these dimensions of home life and of parent-child relationships appeared to be of similar importance to the early reading achievement described in this report* (p. 138).

Durkin's findings have major implications for both parents/caregivers and educators: The children who learn to read early are the ones who have been read to.

In another early study of successful young readers, Clark (1976) observed that a characteristic common to them all was a home environment that was centered around varied experiences and numerous books and magazines. She pointed out that of most importance seemed to be the presence of an interested adult with time to spare to interact in a stimulating, encouraging way. Clark's young subjects displayed above average abilities in auditory memory and sequencing. Being read to and having reading materials in the home have definite positive effects on children's learning. And this proficiency with complex grammatical forms is enhanced with regular oral reading by parents/caregivers at the preschool level (Durkin, 1978; McCormick, 1983).

The research clearly shows that many aspects of reading knowledge are enhanced by reading aloud to children. These skills include the ability to differentiate between the front and back of a book, awareness of the direction in which print is to be read, and an understanding that print provides salient information.

The development of these skills is associated with regular story reading at the preschool level (Durkin, 1974; Teale, 1978). And Freeman and Wasserman (1987) found that the motivation to deal with the process of learning to read is fostered in children who are read to consistently at home.

However children of school age, beginning formal instruction in reading, can also benefit from consistent story reading. Feitelson, Kita, and Goldstein (1986) reported that comprehension skills and the decoding ability of low socioeconomic first grade students read to daily for six months were superior to their control group.

Supported by research which suggests that children's language and literacy development is interwoven and continuous from infancy onward, it is now known that language, literacy, and a love of literature are largely learned at home. As Dorothy Strickland says, "It is very exciting that researchers in various disciplines have recently confirmed the integrated 'birth on' approach long intuitively known by many fine educators" (Strickland & Morrow, 1989).

In light of the importance of early language and literacy development, the role of parents/caregivers cannot be overlooked. There is nothing that can take the place of good role models and exposure to language and literacy in children's early years. When parents/caregivers read to their children at home, their children's later language and reading achievement are positively influenced (Chomsky, 1972; Mason, Peterman, & Kerr, 1989).

But, as another researcher, Toomey, emphatically states, "We need no more studies telling us that involving parents in home reading is a useful strategy. That has already been confirmed" (1986). What educators do need now is more specific information about the most beneficial ways to facilitate this early parental/caregiver reading for each child. That is the main focus of this program.

Why Many Parents/Caregivers Need Assistance With Family Reading

Parents/caregivers play a significant role in preparing their children to read and in supplementing and reinforcing formal reading instruction. However, many parents/caregivers fail to acknowledge their importance as early teachers and role models for their children. A large number of parents/caregivers are willing to participate, but they may not know what to do to help their children or they may lack the confidence in their ability to help their children in the area of reading. And many parents/caregivers are unaware of their potential ability to help their children experience success in school. Further, some educators are unaware of how they can help parents/caregivers to provide help to their children at home. Parents/caregivers have a very great influence on their children's reading growth; they are a valuable educational resource which must be fully tapped.

In our fast-paced and mobile society of today, child rearing and parenting have changed significantly. Many parents/caregivers who do feel capable to support the schooling of their children are unable to do so for other reasons. For example, parents/caregivers who move often or whose children are bussed long distances to school find it difficult to become involved at school, to support their children's teachers, or even to talk with them. They seldom become members of the school community or offer their help in any way. Besides, the mobile family may soon transfer to another locality, and it is hardly worth the effort for them to explore the school and its possibilities for parental participation and involvement.

Due to many parents/caregivers' lack of knowledge about school and learning practices, their busy work schedules, and many conflicting responsibilities, their help and support have dissipated to an inadequate level in many communities. Often, they have granted to the school the sole responsibility of educating their children. Because of the effects this has had on our nation's students, we have recently re-learned that the home/school and teacher/parent partnerships are absolutely necessary to gain maximum achievement for students.

Despite all these difficulties that parents face, educators and parents/caregivers must try to develop a supportive partnership to do what is best for the children. We must rekindle the spirit of partnership that existed between parents/

caregivers and schools in decades past. We need to reconstruct what was taught in the home, the extended family, and by adults in the neighborhood. Then we have to teach those positive practices to the parents/caregivers of today.

There is a need for parents/caregivers to become acquainted with reading techniques, strategies, and home-centered activities. As Burket (1981) points out:

> *. . . in order for parents to help their children in the area of reading, they must be guided or directed in appropriate activities. And in order for the teachers to best guide and inform the parents, the teachers must be guided and informed of ways that will work best in accomplishing this. Many of these activities are already being performed naturally by some parents. However, being aware of their value and their availability would be a tremendous aid to all parents and ultimately, all children . . . .*

Some obvious questions that arise then are: "How can we best get this information on reading aloud to the parents/caregivers who need it?" and "How can we incorporate the parents/caregivers' help?" Darabi (1979) conducted a study to examine the effects of workshops intended to train parents/caregivers in behaviors appropriate for reading a story book to their children. The results of this study indicate that it **is** possible to alter parents/caregivers' story book reading behaviors through workshop meetings. There was some evidence that mothers' behaviors were more amenable to change than fathers'. Also, parents/caregivers' participation in workshops resulted in higher reading readiness gain scores for their children, especially on items pertaining to work discrimination, ability to draw inferences, and ability to recall factual content.

Following is an explanation of the development of just such a workshop, upon which this program is based, and the positive results experienced by the parents/caregivers who participate in this program.

This Program's Development and Benefits

In 1989-1991 I conducted a national Chapter 1 survey at the Center for the Study of Reading at the University of Illinois on what works with at-risk students in reading (Wilken, 1992). In the questionnaire for educators, there were ten questions related to parents/caregivers. The ten questions existed because it had always been my belief that parents/caregivers greatly influence and determine their children's achievement in school by what is done, or not done, in the home in the preschool years. I wondered if teachers across the nation would share these beliefs.

One of the questions on the survey was "To what extent do you believe that a student's home life affects his/her achievement in school?" The verification that 97% of the teachers believed as I did—that parents/caregivers' influence was either "profoundly important" or "one of the most important influences"— prompted me to do something about improving parent/caregivers' skills for their involvement in their children's education. I wanted to draw on my own experiences and efforts throughout my teaching career, but specifically those at Garden Hills Elementary School in Champaign, Illinois, where for eight years I was principal. My own parenting and grandparenting experiences were also invaluable. With this storehouse of expertise, I decided to develop a parents/caregiver education program which focused on reading. In this way, I could make a small contribution to the much larger task of teaching children to learn to read.

I believed then and still believe today that there is a need to recapture some of the helpful prereading experiences in which families were involved in the past. Many of these concepts and skills can be taught to the parents/caregivers of today through a brief, pleasant educational program that focuses on learning how to read with children. This program is based on the principle that parents/caregivers can apply this knowledge while reading with their own children in a ten-minute read-aloud session, five times per week. This enables parents/caregivers to enhance, enrich, and extend their children's learning. In this way, they indeed can become their children's first, most influential, and favorite teachers.

The first step in the development of this parent/caregiver education program was to involve a group of 17 teachers who volunteered for a reading association's service project to educate parents in a program entitled "What to Do When You Read With Children." Dr. Patricia Edwards, author of *Parents As Partners In Reading*, shared with us her experiences in working with parents in Louisiana. We used her book as a resource (Edwards, 1990). I presented several workshops as a member of this volunteer group. I noted that the parents attending had good ideas and suggestions for the program and I documented their suggestions, comments, questions, and evaluations.

Diverse groups attended these early presentations. The audiences were composed of parents/caregivers, teachers (reading and classroom), librarians, teacher and parent aides, and other volunteers. This program today is the result of the input and feedback from those participants as well as my diverse experiences as an elementary teacher and school principal. The program has been constantly and continuously revised to incorporate the suggestions of many more participants over a two and one-half year period.

The purpose of this *Educator/Workshop Leader's Guide* is to teach people to be workshop leaders for *How to Read With Your Children*. These leaders in turn can conduct this program for parents/caregivers in their schools or communities. Some parents/caregivers, after receiving this parent training, might also volunteer to serve as workshop leaders and train other parents/caregivers in their schools or communities.

In 1993, the parent/caregiver program was evaluated by three groups of people. One were a group of 62 teachers who were not familiar with the program, and who evaluated the content. Another were a group of 110 workshop participants who had been trained as leaders of the parent/caregiver education workshop, or as disseminators of the program information. They shared the many ways in which they used the program. (These two groups were represented by more Chapter 1 reading teachers than any other group of educators.) Finally, 41 parents gave their opinions and feedback about the program after they had worked with the educators who had received the workshop training.

The responses that follow present educators' approval of the program as developed. They indicate their varied and many uses of the program and how it helped them to educate parents about the importance of reading with young children. Most important, the responses following present the parents/caregivers' approval of the program, and the help they and their children received from the program information.

Table 1 details the specific information that workshop leaders disseminated to parents/caregivers. All of these topics are included in the outline in Section Two of this guide, and you may wish to take these other workshop leaders' priorities into consideration when planning your own workshop(s).

TABLE 1
What Information Was Disseminated by Educators/Workshop Leaders?

Why parents/caregivers should read to their children	68%
What parents/caregivers can do with their children before, during, and after they read together	55%
What positive comments parents/caregivers can make while they read with their children	45%
How parents/caregivers and their children can choose what to read	43%
What parents/caregivers can do to connect reading with writing for their children	37%
What parents/caregivers can do when they do not have books to read with their children	35%
Where parents/caregivers should read with their children	35%
What specific knowledge children can learn from parents/caregivers during reading	32%

Although conducting workshops is probably the most effective and direct way to disseminate this important reading information to parents/caregivers, there are many other ways (as shown in Table 2) that you might consider using this information in addition to or instead of workshop presentation(s).

TABLE 2
How the Information Was Disseminated by Educators/Workshop Leaders

Discussion with friends, relatives, educators, and others	59%
Discussions with parents/caregivers at parent/teacher conference time about the importance of reading with their children	43%
Planning to disseminate this information to parents/caregivers in conferences, classroom and school newsletters, school news in newspapers, by radio, etc.	39%
Reading with their own children or grandchildren at home	38%
A workshop/program for parents/caregivers at school	36%
A handout containing some of the information given to parents/caregivers at school conferences or meetings	35%
Discussions with parents/caregivers in an informal meeting—such as at the grocery store, playground/park, or a school activity—about the importance of reading with their children	35%

A school or classroom newsletter containing some of the information 34%
A memo to parents/caregivers containing some of the information 29%
A workshop/program for parents/caregivers somewhere other than the
    school 15%
In-home training of parents/caregivers on how to read with their
    children 14%
Reading with young children in a daycare or preschool situation 8%
A handout for (reading methods) college students containing some of
    the information 3%

Finally, Table 3 summarizes what parents who attended the workshop say they learned from the presentations. Following Table 3 are some instructions for using this program that will enable you to experience the same (or better!) positive results with the parents of your students or in your school community.

TABLE 3
What Parents Learned

I Learned:	Strongly Agree	Agree	Neutral	Disagree
Reading to my child is important for many reasons.	78%	17%	5%	0%
What to do when I read to my child.	61%	37%	0%	2%
Who I can ask to help me choose books for my child.	43%	53%	5%	0%
I am my child's first and most influential teacher	68%	27%	0%	4%
I should, and I do try, to read to my child for ten or more minutes per day, five times per week.	65%	33%	3%	0%
What to do with my child that will help her/him to learn to read when we do not have books to read.	54%	34%	12%	0%

How to Use This Program

▬ Goals for the Program

For the Workshop Leader . . .

- Create an awareness in parents/caregivers that they are their children's first and favorite teachers.

- Create an awareness in parents/caregivers that they are their children's most important and influential teachers.

- Improve parents/caregivers' knowledge of strategies, activities, and techniques that support their children's interest in reading and motivation to learn to read or to become the best reader possible.

- Create and present additional activities that will encourage parents/caregivers to continuously and consistently read with their children.

- Gain satisfaction from disseminating important information that will benefit both parents/caregivers and their children.

For the Parents/Caregivers . . .

- Enjoy reading with their children.

- Develop in their children an enjoyment of and love for reading.

- Develop their children's imagination and creativity through family reading.

- Enhance the children's learning opportunities through family reading.

- Identify or develop a suitable family reading environment.

- Implement and/or create activities that develop their children's interest in reading and other academic subjects.

- Develop an awareness in their children that reading and writing are connected.

For the Preschool/Primary Grade Children . . .

- ◆ Gain a love for reading, and the motivation to learn to read or to become the best reader possible.

- ◆ Talk about and enjoy the books and other materials they read at home.

- ◆ Talk about and enjoy their parents/caregivers' reading with them.

- ◆ Check out more books from the school, classroom, or public library.

- ◆ Listen to their teachers read stories, poems, and books with greater interest.

- ◆ Talk about and bring reading "artifacts" to school, such as letters, art work, poems, and stories that were created at home.

- ◆ Ask questions and make comments more often about what is read in the classroom, at daycare, or at home.

- ◆ Understand that there is a connection between reading and writing.

Who Can Be a Workshop Leader?

Many people have shared the information in *How to Read With Your Children* in a variety of ways. These people were from diverse cultural, ethnic, and racial groups; from a variety of backgrounds and experiences; and from a wide range of educational levels. Some taught parents/caregivers in their homes, and some taught groups of two to 20 parents/caregivers in a workshop setting. Some individuals taught non-English speaking parents/caregivers in their native tongues.

Volunteers from all walks of life can present the information in this program:

- ◆ Stay-at-home and working mothers/fathers

- ◆ Grandmothers and grandfathers

- ◆ K-6 classroom teachers

- ◆ Resource room or special education teachers

- ◆ Chapter 1 teachers and aides

- ◆ PTA or other parent organization participants

- ◆ Head Start aides and teachers

- ◆ Librarians (both school and public)

- Library aides (both school and public)

- Preschool teachers and other early childhood educators

- Daycare staff

- School administrators

- Family literacy personnel

- Intergenerational literacy personnel

- Other various volunteers and organization members

I encourage and challenge you as an educator to share this information with parents.

Who Can Attend the Workshop(s)?

- Parents/caregivers of any preschool or primary grade student

- Parents/caregivers from preschools and daycare centers

- Parents/caregivers from elementary school PTA and/or other parent organizations or groups

- Head Start parents/caregivers

- Members of church-sponsored groups

- Members of service club groups

- Members of neighborhood groups

- Members of public and subsidized housing groups

- Members of library-sponsored groups (either school or public)

- Members of family and intergenerational groups

- Senior citizen and/or grandparent volunteers

- Reading methods college students

- Any other volunteers who want to read with children, such as service clubs and civic organizations

▬▬ When Can the Workshop(s) Be Held?

Workshops can be held during the day or evening, on weekdays and on weekends, including Sundays. Workshops can be held during school or church hours, when the children are attending their classes. The educator/workshop leader will know the group best. If the participants are parents who do not work outside the home, then the workshop(s) could be held during the day. If the participants are working parents, an evening meeting would be better. The educator/workshop leader might consider surveying the parents/caregivers before scheduling the workshop time(s). For example:

> *I would like to meet (check appropriate times):*
>   ___ morning   ___ afternoon   ___ evening
>
> *The days of the week I prefer (circle all appropriate):*
>
>   Sun.   Mon.   Tues.   Wed.   Thurs.   Fri.   Sat.

The length of sessions can vary, although one of the following schedules have been found to work best:

- ◆ 1 three-hour session
- ◆ 2 one and one-half hour sessions
- ◆ 3 one-hour sessions

A sample agenda for each of these three options is provided in Section Two of this guide.

▬▬ Where Can the Workshop(s) Be Held?

The workshop(s) should be held where it is convenient for parents/caregivers to attend. If a workshop is sponsored by a preschool, a daycare facility, or an elementary school, meeting there might be most appropriate. However, if a workshop is conducted in a housing complex, there is usually a community room which can be used. If a church is sponsoring a workshop, the members would probably host the group there. Meeting in a participant's home in a neighborhood is also a possibility. Where transportation is not readily available, this is a good alternative. Recreation centers, parks district facilities, or a city building are other meeting location possibilities. Many public libraries also have meeting space available to the public.

How Do I Conduct a Workshop?

To prepare for conducting a workshop on this program, first read your copy of the *Parent/Caregiver's Guide* of *How to Read With Your Children*. Each workshop participant should also have and bring with them a copy of this guide. (This resource has been intentionally kept affordable so that parents/caregivers can purchase them individually or so that schools/organizations can provide them to participants.)

After deciding upon a date, time, location, and format (one, two, or three sessions) of the workshop, you must communicate this information to parents/caregivers. You might also choose to register interested participants for the workshop. There is a "publicity packet" that will serve these purposes provided for your convenience in Section Three of this guide. Give the participants an agenda (provided for you in Section Two of this guide) either when they register or at the beginning of the workshop session(s).

Limit each workshop group to no more than 20 people, and arrange the meeting room so that it is conducive to the exchange of information (with all the participants visible to one another). If the group numbers ten to 20, a circle of tables with the workshop leader at the top of the circle seated at or standing beside a table is appropriate. If the group numbers less than ten, groups of three to four participants at three tables, with the leader at a smaller table at the head of the group, is an appropriate arrangement. Again the participants should face one another, and be within conversation distance to one another.

The workshop leader should be present to meet each participant as all arrive. A name badge should be made for each participant, and presented to them on arrival. Be sure to wear a name badge yourself, as well. If the meeting place is a school, the school mascot, emblem, or logo should be reproduced on the name badges. This gives the group an identity, and the idea that they are contributing to their children's education at the school.

To actually disseminate the program information, use any or all of the outline provided in Section Two of this guide (depending upon the session format and agenda you've selected). The outline makes reference to specific pages in the *Parent/Caregiver's Guide*. You will need to be sure to bring your copy with you to the workshop session(s). It will also be helpful for you to highlight or otherwise "flag" in your copy of the guide the pertinent points you will address during the workshop presentation(s).

Some points in the presentation outline make reference to "Parent/Caregiver Handouts." The reproducible masters for these handouts are found at the end of the outline. You will need to prepare beforehand photocopies of any of these handouts you wish to incorporate into your presentation. Note also that any or all of these handouts could be prepared as overhead transparency masters if you wish to use an overhead projector and have this equipment available to you.

At the end of the workshop session (or at a later date, as appropriate), conduct one or more of the "additional activities" provided after the presentation outline, if possible. Be sure to allow time for a question and answer session after the workshop presentation, and to thank the participants for their time and attention.

(**Note:** Please feel free to contact the author about your experiences in leading *How to Read With Your Children* Workshops, and any ideas/comments you may have: Phyllis A. Wilken, 2022 Bentbrook Road, Champaign, Illinois 61821; (217) 356-6877; FAX (217) 244-4501)

Tips for Successful Workshops

- Serve beverages and a snack during the presentation or during a break in the presentation. These might be donated by a local grocer, by a fast food restaurant, or by a PTA or parent organization or service club.

- Provide babysitting services, at the workshop location, for parents/caregivers who need it.

- If children **are** brought to the workshop, they could be included at the end of the session for a story reading by the workshop leader. This is an excellent way to model the art of story reading that the participants just heard about and discussed, and is enjoyable for the children!

- Begin and end the session on time.

- Provide the parent/caregiver participants with an agenda (see Section Two of this guide).

- Allow time for the parents/caregivers to ask you questions.

- Allow time for the parents/caregivers to mingle with one another and exchange ideas.

- Remember and respect the fact that you may know more about reading, but the parents/caregivers know their children and family needs better than you! (Don't preach or lecture.)

- Be sensitive to the needs/interests of your audience, and flexible in your delivery. If the parent/caregiver participants are especially interested in certain topics, and not very interested in others, be willing to adjust the time you've allotted for each. Likewise, if the parents/caregivers are expressing boredom (through their words, facial expressions, or body language), pick up the pace!

- Realize that some parents/caregivers with low literacy or English language skills, or with prohibitive time constraints, may have difficulty reading all the suggestions in the *Parent/Caregiver's Guide* to *How to Read With Your Children*. These participants will need you to review with them many of the ideas in that guide.

- Realize that some parents/caregivers who are proficient in English, and with high literacy skills and the time to read themselves, will expect you to "add value" to the *Parent/Caregiver's Guide* during your presentation. They will need you to supplement the information contained in that guide with some additional ideas and examples (such as those provided in the outline in Section Two of this guide). Otherwise, they may think to themselves, "Why am I here? I've already read this!"

- Use humor whenever possible, and enjoy presenting this valuable information.

- Emphasize to the parents/caregivers that **any** parent can use this program—it requires no prior experience or education level, and minimal resources.

- Emphasize to the parents/caregivers that reading to their children will be a pleasurable activity their family will enjoy, not simply another "chore" on their "to do list." It is an opportunity for the parents/caregivers to nurture and cuddle their children; to give individual attention to their children; to make positive remarks about their children's listening and comprehension; and an opportunity to share their values, morals, and beliefs with their children. Thoroughly highlight the benefits of family reading for both the parents/caregivers and their children.

- A fun activity at the end of a workshop session is to hold a drawing for a free children's book(s) (new, used, or donated), or other door prizes for both the parents/caregivers and the children. If you choose to include a drawing at the end of the workshop session(s), you will need to either prepare slips of paper with all the participants' names on them beforehand, or have the participants enter their own names as they arrive.

Section Two

Conducting the Workshop(s)

Three Sample Agendas

Following are sample agendas for each of the three recommended workshop formats:

- 1 three-hour session

- 2 one and one-half hour sessions

- 3 one-hour sessions

The times have been left blank for you to customize to your needs. As a guide, the suggested time durations have been indicated in the left column. These are provided simply for your convenience. You may, of course, customize them to your liking.

A G E N D A

How to Read With Your Children

Three-Hour Session

(15 minutes) . . . _____ to _____

    I. Introductions of workshop leader and participants

(25 minutes) . . . _____ to _____

    II. Goals for the Parent/Caregiver Program

    III. Why Many Parents/Caregivers Don't Read to Their Children

IV. Principles of the Program

    V. Background Information on Reading

(15 minutes) . . . _____ to _____ **Break**

    Refreshments available

(45 minutes) . . . _____ to _____

    VI. Why Read to Your Child?

    VII. What to Do at Home to Prepare Your Child for School

    VIII. How to Select Books for Your Child

    IX. What to Do When You Do Not Have Books to Read

(15 minutes) . . . _____ to _____ **Break**

    Refreshments available

(55 minutes) . . . _____ to _____

    X. Where and When to Read With Your Child

    XI. How to Read With Your Child

    XII. Positive Comments That Can Be Made to Your Child

    XIII. How to Make the Reading/Writing Connection

(10 minutes) . . . _____ to _____

    XIV. Conclusion

A G E N D A

How to Read With Your Children

One and One-Half Hour Sessions

F i r s t   S e s s i o n

(15 minutes) . . . _____ to _____

    I. Introduction of workshop leader and participants

(25 minutes) . . . _____ to _____

    II. Goals for the Parent/Caregiver Program

    III. Why Many Parents/Caregivers Don't Read to Their Children

    IV. Principles of the Program

    V. Background Information on Reading

(15 minutes) . . . _____ to _____ **Break**

    Refreshments available

(25 minutes) . . . _____ to _____

    VI. Why Read to Your Child?

    VII. What to Do at Home to Prepare Your Child for School

    VIII. How to Select Books for Your Child

(10 minutes) . . . _____ to _____ **First Session Conclusion**

    Questions and answers

    Brief discussion of second session

A G E N D A

How to Read With Your Children

One and One-Half Hour Sessions

S e c o n d   S e s s i o n

(10 minutes) . . . _____ to _____   **Session Open**

Parents/caregivers volunteer to share their experiences with implementing a workshop idea, or from a family reading session, since the last workshop session.

(25 minutes) . . . _____ to _____

    IX. What to Do When You Do Not Have Books to Read

    X. Where and When to Read to Your Child

(15 minutes) . . . _____ to _____   **Break**

    Refreshments available

(25 minutes) . . . _____ to _____

    XI. How to Read With Your Child

    XII. Positive Comments That Can Be Made to Your Child

    XIII. How to Make the Reading/Writing Connection

(15 minutes) . . . _____ to _____

    XIV. Conclusion

A G E N D A

How to Read With Your Children

One Hour Sessions

F i r s t   S e s s i o n

(15 minutes) . . . _____ to _____

   I. Introduction of workshop leader and participants

(10 minutes) . . . _____ to _____

   II. Goals for the Parent/Caregiver Program

   III. Why Many Parents/Caregivers Don't Read to Their Children

(10 minutes) . . . _____ to _____ **Break**

Refreshments available

(15 minutes) . . . _____ to _____

   IV. Principles of the Program

   V. Background Information on Reading

(10 minutes) . . . _____ to _____ **First Session Conclusion**

Questions and answers

Brief discussion of second session

S e c o n d   S e s s i o n

(10 minutes) . . . _____ to _____ **Session Open**

Parents/caregivers volunteer to share their experiences with implementing a workshop idea, or from a family reading session, since the last workshop session.

(15 minutes) . . . _____ to _____

   VI. Why Read to Your Child?

   VII. What to Do at Home to Prepare Your Child for School

   VIII. How to Select Books for Your Child

One Hour Sessions

(c o n t i n u e d)

(10 minutes) . . . _____ to _____   **Break**

Refreshments available

(25 minutes) . . . _____ to _____

IX. What to Do When You Do Not Have Books to Read

X. Where and When to Read to Your Child

(10 minutes) . . . _____ to _____   **Second Session Conclusion**

Questions and answers

Brief discussion of third session

T h i r d   S e s s i o n

(10 minutes) . . . _____ to _____   **Session Open**

Parents/caregivers volunteer to share their experiences with implementing a workshop idea, or from a family reading session, since the last workshop session.

(20 minutes) . . . _____ to _____

XI. How to Read With Your Child

XII. Positive Comments That Can Be Made to Your Child

(10 minutes) . . . _____ to _____   **Break**

Refreshments available

(5 minutes) . . . . _____ to _____

XIII. How to Make the Reading/Writing Connection

(15 minutes) . . . _____ to _____

XIV. Conclusion

Outline of Workshop Information

I.   **Introduction**

NOTES:

A.   Introduce yourself, giving as much or little information as you feel is appropriate.

B.   Ask all the parent/caregiver participants to introduce themselves to the group (standing up not necessary), sharing the following information:

   ♦   Name

   ♦   Number of children in the family and their ages/grade levels

   ♦   How long their child/children has/have attended this school (church, daycare center, etc.)

   ♦   What she/he hopes to gain by attending this workshop

   ♦   What neighborhood the family lives in, such as number of blocks east, west, north, or south of the school (preschool, etc.)

(**Note:** Parents/caregivers may learn from this exchange of information that their children live near other participants' children and could play together after school hours, who some of their neighbors are, and who might live nearby and willing to exchange babysitting services.)

C. Reinforce for the parents/caregivers that they are likely already doing many of the recommendations they will hear about in the workshop session, and that that is commendable. Emphasize that many parents/caregivers have already formed a good foundation for family reading.

D. Tell the participants that they will also learn some new information and ideas about family reading sessions, and that you hope they will put into practice at least three things they learn at this session.

E. Distribute and review the agenda for the session. Explain that you will answer the parents/caregivers' questions, if they are not addressed during the workshop presentation, at the end of the planned presentation.

F. Encourage the participants to spend time talking with one another during the break(s), as well as viewing any materials on display (library books, etc.). Remind them that they are also welcome to speak with you individually if they have specific questions they don't wish to share with the whole group. Tell the participants that the break(s) cannot run longer than ten to 15 minutes (as appropriate) if the session is to end on time, but there will be additional time for questions and for meeting others at the end of the session.

II. Goals for the Parent/Caregiver Program

    A. Distribute Parent/Caregiver Handout 1.

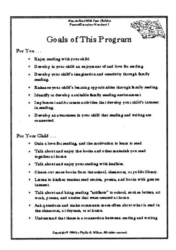

    B. Emphasize the many benefits for both the parents/caregivers and their children. Focus on how family reading creates a special, positive time with their children, while also helping to meet their young learners' academic needs.

    C. Ask if anyone can think of any other benefits/ goals for either the parents/caregivers or the children that are not listed on Handout 1. If so, have everyone record these additions on their own copy of Handout 1.

III. Why Many Parents/Caregivers Don't Read to Their Children

    A. Refer to pages 7-10 of the *Parent/ Caregiver's Guide* to *How to Read With Your Children*. (These sound answers to the five most common reasons offered by other parents for not reading to their children were prepared in hopes of encouraging parents/ caregivers to read aloud to their children on a regular basis.)

B. Briefly review the responses to each of the five reasons. Then ask if any participant still believes that any one of the five reasons has not been sufficiently addressed to convince her/him to read to her/his child.

If this is the case, have the whole group brainstorm a response or responses to help this participant remove this impediment to reading for her/his family. (This should be done in a supportive, nonconfrontational way!)

C. Ask if any participant has any other reason he/she believes is cause not to read to his/her child.

If another unique reason is offered, discuss as a group a positive response to the reason offered.

IV. Principles of the Program

A. Refer to page 15 of the *Parent/Caregiver's Guide* to *How to Read With Your Children*.

B. Answer any questions the parents/caregivers might have about the procedures. For example:

♦ "What happens if we aren't able to read all five times in a week?"

♦ "What if we can only read for five minutes one night?"

♦ "How can I be sure to notice when my child's reading performance is improving?"

♦ Etc.

C. Show the participants a sample reading time recording system, either for your child or a fictional child. For example, show a calendar with simple notations of reading times for one month.

Emphasize that this does not have to be complicated, and should not be perceived as "cumbersome paperwork" that might discourage a parent/caregiver from implementing family reading.

(**Note:** A free yearly calendar—such as a wall calendar with local nature scenes from an insurance company or auto dealership, or better yet, one with a "child-like" motif donated from a local children's bookstore— makes a great door prize for workshop participants!)

V. **Background Information on Reading**

A. Discuss the many societal changes and technological developments since the World War II era that make it challenging for parents/caregivers to meet their children's reading readiness, language, and other academic needs.

Factors to address might include:

◆ Household technology such as TVs, VCRs, home video games, telephones and cellular phones, computers and online services, etc. usurp family interaction time.

◆ Fast and frozen foods decrease family meal times, and therefore the opportunity for family discussions.

NOTES:

◆ American families today are mobile/
transient both by economic necessity
and by choice.

◆ The spiraling divorce rate and increase
in the number of single-parent families
leave many single parents "stretched
thin" on time.

◆ The majority of parents today work
outside of the home, placing more
young children in sometimes
educationally-impoverished daycare
situations. (This is not a condemnation
of working mothers, simply a factor that
those in our society must better
compensate for!)

◆ Many parents today are raising their
families without the proximity and/or
support of their extended families.

◆ Many working parents/caregivers often
don't have the flexibility and/or time to
participate in traditional school events,
organizations, and activities, and depend
upon the schools to solely educate their
children without their support or assistance.

B. Distribute Parent/Caregiver Handout 2.

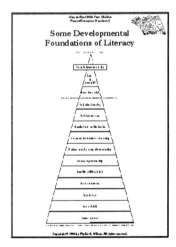

C. Discuss the importance of concept awareness. Discussing sizes (big, little, etc.),
shapes (circles, squares, etc.), colors (red,
blue, etc.), in and out, to and from, etc., all
help children to understand words they
encounter in reading. This is often re-
ferred to as the developing and understanding of language, or what people say
when they talk with one another (the
bottom three tiers on the pyramid).
Many children's books focus on these
concepts, and give children the practice
they need to understand these concepts
and begin to develop their language
skills.

D. Discuss what children do in the beginning
stages of reading. Children may at a very
early age, even before they say a word,
point to pictures in a picture book. This is
an indication that they want the adult to
say the name of the animal or thing that is
pictured on the page. Children may mimic
adults' reading in the early stages of talking by saying the names of characters or
words connected to pictures. Later, when
their talking is more fluent and recogniz-
able, they may page through a familiar
book telling the story as they remember it.
Sometimes children even turn the pages
of a story book at the right time when
being read to. These are all positive signs
that the children are showing an interest
in reading. All these early efforts should
be praised and encouraged.

E. Discuss how families prepare preschool and primary grade children for reading. Reading readiness ideas to address might include:

- ◆ Developing language and verbal skills through family conversations.

- ◆ Providing an environment and experiences where love, caring, and concern prevail.

- ◆ Talking with their children and modeling/explaining the emotions of joy, anger, disappointment, sadness, and surprise.

- ◆ Providing many varied experiences that extend their children's knowledge and interests, such as . . .

  - Trips to a zoo, a museum, fairs, festivals, theatre productions, etc.

  - Walks in their neighborhood and parks to observe plants, animals, birds, and the weather.

  - Trips to pet stores, pet shows, bicycle shops, shopping malls, farms, sporting events, etc.

  - Planting a garden.

  - Going to the grocery store and talking about all the items they see, where they came from, their color, shape, etc.

  - Reading books, stories, comics, and other reading materials with their children.

  - Telling their children stories and dramatizing them.

- Providing creative activities such as creating, writing, and illustrating stories.

- Providing writing opportunities to illustrate the reading/writing connection.

- Playing board and card games with individual children and with all the children in the family.

- Including all the children in the family while reading and discussing a story or book. The children can learn from one another in this way.

- Providing time for singing songs, memorizing nursery rhymes, doing finger plays, and skipping and clapping to music.

- Following a simple recipe, preparing the food together, and serving and eating it with family members.

- Talking about billboards and signs, traffic signals and road signs, store displays, and trucks and other machinery while riding in the car.

- Carrying books to read while waiting in a doctor's office, while waiting for a family member, while at the laundromat, etc.

(**Note**: Some of these ideas are presented throughout the *Parent/Caregiver's Guide*, but this list provides a "warm-up" and introduction to those topics.)

F. Ask the parents/caregivers what they would like to learn about prereading and reading with their children. (This will help you to focus the presentation of the next eight topics to best suit the needs of the participants.) If possible, write their comments on a chalkboard, white board, overhead transparency, or large piece of paper for all the participants to see.

VI. **Why Read to Your Child?**

A. Refer to pages 23-25 of the *Parent/Caregiver's Guide* to *How to Read With Your Children*.

B. Emphasize and clarify a few of the reasons in each of the three categories ("Social Reasons," "Academic Reasons," and "Parent/Caregiver Reasons"), as well as the "Summary Box."

C. Ask the participants to share their own reasons for reading with (or wanting to read with) their children. Have everyone record any new ideas that they agree with in their own copy of the guide.

D. Suggest to the participants that they save their children's favorite books for future grandchildren. Their children will appreciate this foresight when they have these books to use in their own family reading sessions with the next generation (as described on page 20 of the *Parent/Caregiver's Guide*).

VII. **What to Do at Home to Prepare Your Child for School**

A. Refer to pages 31-35 of the *Parent/ Caregiver's Guide* to *How to Read With Your Children*.

B. Emphasize and clarify a few of the ideas in each of the three categories ("language skills," "specific facts about reading," and "after reading a story or book"), as well as the "Summary Box."

C. Distribute Parent/Caregiver Handout 3.

D. To reinforce the notion that ideas for early childhood learning experiences are seemingly endless, have the participants as a group quickly think of at least 20 other ideas not already listed on pages 31-35 of the *Parent/Caregiver's Guide*. As the suggestions are called out, have everyone record them on their own copy of Handout 3.

Some suggestions to get the group started include:

NOTES:

- Watch the television program "Sesame Street" (still running on PBS stations) together, and provide opportunities for the child to practice the number and letter taught in the program throughout the rest of the day.

- Count to ten (or 50, or 100, as age-appropriate) together, alternating responses (child, adult, child, etc.).

- Sing the "Alphabet Song" together.

- Play "Simon Says," prompting the child to practice concepts such as "up," "down," "left," "right," "behind," "on top," etc.

- Provide the child a set of alphabet refrigerator magnets. Mix the magnets up, and have the child re-alphabetize them.

- Look at a different letter's book in an encyclopedia set each day, together learning the names of ten things that begin with "A," "B," etc.

- Jump rope with the child, counting the skips. Or create your own jump rope rhymes.

- Have the child sort blocks, toys, books, etc. by color or size.

- Write "secret messages" in a coded language (e.g., A=26, B=25, C=24, etc.) for the child to decipher.

- Teach the child the Manual Alphabet (pictured in books on American Sign Language), useful for both learning the alphabet and communicating with others who have hearing impairments.

VIII. How to Select Books for Your Child

A. Refer to pages 41-42 of the *Parent/Caregiver's Guide* to *How to Read With Your Children*.

B. Emphasize and clarify a few of the ways to select books, and the "Summary Box."

C. Distribute to each participant an application form for a library card for her/his child. (Have extra forms available for parents/caregivers with more than one child, and for themselves as well!) Tell the participants pertinent information such as the location and operating times of the local public library, minimum age of children to be issued a library card, maximum number of books (if any) that may be checked out, late fines that will be imposed for overdue books, and dates/times of regularly scheduled children's story hours, etc.

Encourage the participants to become frequent patrons of their local library, and to obtain library cards in their children's names, if they have not already done so. Giving children their own cards emphasizes the importance and value of reading, and encourages their active participation in, responsibility for, and "ownership" of the process.

D. Provide and distribute a list or lists of book titles appropriate for preschool, kindergarten, grade 1, grade 2, and grade 3 children. You can create this list or lists with the help of a local children's library librarian, or through one of the methods detailed in the *Parent/Caregiver's Guide*. This will help to make the participants' first (or next) trip to the library with their children easier by giving them a starting point for selecting books.

IX. What to Do When You Do Not Have Books to Read

A. Refer to pages 47-49 of the *Parent/ Caregiver's Guide* to *How to Read With Your Children*.

B. Emphasize and clarify a few of the alternative reading period activities, as well as the "Summary Box."

C. Ask if any parent/caregiver participants would have difficulty obtaining any of the "environmental print" sources listed on page 47. As a group, brainstorm other unique sources of "environmental print" materials for family reading sessions (for example: school newsletters, older siblings' already-graded school papers, greeting cards, papers from the parent/ caregiver's work place, etc.) Have everyone record in their own copy of the guide any ideas that appeal to them.

D. Give the participants a quick and simple example of how environmental print can be educational for their children. Hold up a popular cereal box, and demonstrate a few things they could ask their own children to do using such a box. These activities might include:

- Name everything pictured on the box.

- Name all the colors of the box.

- Name all the different shapes of things on the box.

- Count the total number of items pictured on the box.

- Find all the numbers printed on the box, in sequence, beginning with 1.

- Find all the letters of the alphabet possible, in sequence, beginning with A.

E. If time allows, give the participants a hands-on experience of using environmental print. Ask the participants to introduce themselves to the others around them, and to split into groups of two to three. Give each small group a lunch bag or "baggie" with five to ten pictures and words cut from a store flier, magazine, or catalog. (Be sure to include a clipping of a person in every bag.) Explain where the clippings came from, and ask each group to quickly (within, say, one to three minutes) create a story together incorporating the pictures and words they've been provided.

When they've finished, ask one or two volunteer groups to share their story with the whole groups. These silly stories will probably elicit some laughs, and will demonstrate how fun these sorts of reading readiness activities can be.

F. Have available for the participants to look at copies of popular children's periodicals such as *Highlights for Children.* (Many of these periodicals may be checked out from a local children's library.) Also have subscription information handy, and copies of subscription cards, if possible. Encourage the parents/caregivers to supplement their children's reading with such resources.

(**Note:** If you can arrange to have funds donated, a paid subscription to a children's periodical is a much appreciated door prize for workshop participants!)

X. **Where and When to Read With Your Child**

A. Refer to page 55 of the *Parent/Caregiver's Guide* to *How to Read With Your Children.*

B. Emphasize and clarify a couple of the time and location suggestions, as well as the "Summary Box."

C. Offer a few other points for the participants to consider, such as the following:

   ◆ Room temperature is also a factor in creating a pleasant reading environment. If the room is chilly, this may be distracting to a child. If the room is too warm, this may make the child drowsy.

NOTES:

♦ Some research supports the theory that classical music (such as Mozart) softly playing in the background aids in concentration, and in the acquisition of cognitive skills by young children.

♦ Sometimes, for whatever reason, a suitable reading environment cannot be found within the home on a regular basis. But this should not preclude family reading! Some alternative locations for family reading might include:

- Parked in the family vehicle

- At a relative or family friend's house

- In the yard or park in nice weather

- In the child's classroom, preschool, or daycare center after the other children have left for the day or before they arrive in the morning

- In a local library's reading areas

D. Have the group as a whole brainstorm at least three other reading times and locations, and have everyone record in their own copy of the guide the new ideas they think would be helpful to their family.

XI. How to Read With Your Child

A. Refer to pages 61-63 of the *Parent/Caregiver's Guide* to *How to Read With Your Children*.

B. Emphasize and clarify a few of the procedures in each of the three categories ("before reading," "while reading," and "after reading"), as well as the "Summary Box."

C. Point out that the most possibilities for enriching the reading experience occur after the story or book has been read, and thus that list is the longest. Encourage the parents/caregivers to allow plenty of time for discussion with their children after their reading.

D. Tell the participants that another post-reading idea is to have their children re-tell them, from memory, the story after it has been read. This demonstrates comprehension and attention to the reading, and may elicit story discussion topics.

E. Distribute Parent/Caregiver Handout 4. Explain that although many of these points are provided throughout the *Parent/ Caregiver's Guide*, Handout 4 is an excellent summation of the main print awareness concepts their children should learn from family reading sessions.

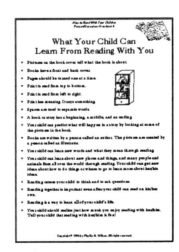

F. Tell the participants how they can extend the concept that books are written by people called authors, and that the pictures in books are created by people called illustrators, by showing their children how one can search for books using these people's names through the computers commonly available for library patrons in most public libraries today. For example, most of these cataloging computers will allow one to search for books by subject, title, or author with only a few simple keystrokes.

This activity can also lead to many other discussion topics for parents/caregivers and their children, such as the alphabetizing of books on library shelves by author, how books are grouped as fiction and non-fiction, and so on as age-appropriate.

XII. Positive Comments That Can Be Made to Your Child

A. Refer to pages 67-70 of the *Parent/Caregiver's Guide* to *How to Read With Your Children*.

B. Emphasize and clarify a few of the general and specific types of comments in each of the three categories ("before reading," "while reading," and "after the reading"), as well as the "Summary Box."

C. Distribute Parent/Caregiver Handout 5.

D. Challenge the participants to think of one positive comment/praise statement that begins with each letter of the alphabet, by brainstorming as a group. As the comments are called out, have everyone jot down on their copy of Handout 5 any statements they would like to use with their child.

(**Note:** Here are some examples to get the group started—"Awesome!"; "Beautiful reading"; "Check out who's ready for reading!"; "Delightful listening"; "Excellent!"; etc.)

XIII. How to Make the Reading/Writing Connection

A. Refer to pages 75-76 of the *Parent/ Caregiver's Guide* to *How to Read With Your Children*.

B. Emphasize and clarify a few of the suggestions, as well as the "Summary Box."

NOTES:

C. Distribute Parent/Caregiver Handout 6. Tell the participants that these pages can be photocopied as often as desired, and then cut up into flash cards for use as described on pages 72-73 of the *Parent/Caregiver's Guide*.

D. Explain that the two flash card pages can be photocopied back-to-back so that the children can also write and/or illustrate the words on the backs of the cards they've answered correctly.

XIV. Conclusion

A. Ask the parent/caregiver participants if they have any other questions, and address those as appropriate.

B. Distribute Parent/Caregiver Handout 7.

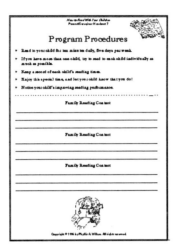

C. Review the principles of the program with the participants again, ensuring that they all have the simple steps down pat and are motivated to begin them!

D. If appropriate, tell the participants how they can contact you with any additional questions after they begin implementing the program with their families at home. Have them write your contact information on their own copy of Handout 7.

Also encourage them to exchange addresses and telephone numbers with other parents/caregivers they met during the workshop. Keeping in touch with other participants can help keep them on track with family reading through the "moral support" of their peers.

E. If you are holding a drawing for a door prize or prizes, now is the appropriate time to select the winning names.

F. If you wish, have a "Workshop Evaluation Form" available to the participants at the end of the session, and encourage them to give you feedback. (A form is provided for your convenience in Section Three of this guide.)

XV. Additional Activities

If time allows, you might consider supplementing the presentation outline with one or more of the following activities. These can be done at the end of a workshop session, or at a later, prearranged time:

♦ Have a school librarian, a primary grade teacher who keeps abreast of children's books and literature, or a person who orders books for children in a book store or department store speak to the parents/caregivers on criteria for selecting books. The speaker could recommend books for different age groups, and could provide books for the parents/caregivers to review.

♦ Show the parents/caregivers a videotape on reading that is available from libraries, schools, or educational service centers. Or the school may wish to purchase such a tape. (Suitable videotapes are available with *Parents As Partners In Reading* [Edwards, 1990].)

♦ Have a pediatrician, general practitioner medical doctor, public health worker, pediatric nurse, child development specialist, or early childhood/preschool educator speak to the parents/caregivers on the physical, emotional, and social development of children and what part parents/caregivers play in their children's learning at school.

NOTES:

♦ Invite a teacher from each grade level represented by the participating parents/caregivers' children to relate and discuss the reading expectancies for each grade level. Ask the teachers to bring examples of grade-level reading materials. An average child's writing sample should also be presented for each grade (with the children's names removed).

These materials could be displayed afterwards on a table where parents/caregivers can see the development of handwriting as well as read the creative writings of an average reader at their children's grade level. The reading materials, labeled for each grade, would also be displayed. It should be emphasized, however, that children may be at different developmental stages even though they are the same age/in the same grade.

♦ Offer a literacy class/tutoring for non-English speaking or adult nonreaders at the school, through a community college, or through an adult literacy or adult education program.

♦ Organize a Family Reading Club for the parent/caregiver participants, or for the school as a whole. (Information and forms for a Family Reading Club are provided in Appendix II of the *Parent/Caregiver's Guide* to *How to Read With Your Children*.)

♦ Organize a Reading Partners program for the parent/caregiver participants, or for the school as a whole. Information and a volunteer letter for the Reading Partners program are provided in Appendix III of the *Parent/Caregiver's Guide* to *How to Read With Your Children*.)

NOTES:

XVI. If Children Are Present at the Workshop

If children are present at the workshop, and you and the parents/caregivers wish to include them rather than providing babysitting services, any of the following optional activities can be incorporated into the presentation outline:

◆ A second or third workshop session could begin with a "sharing time." Parents/caregivers and their children could share the best book or story they have read since the last workshop session. They could show everyone the book and briefly summarize the story. Or a parent/caregiver can volunteer to read (or you can read) one of these favorite stories or books. Then the child can share why he/she liked the book and the character he/she liked best and why. This discussion can be a model for parents/caregivers to implement while reading at home.

◆ Various activities might be arranged in which parents/caregivers and their children work together. Always popular creative activities involving reading and writing focus on holidays and the seasons. For holiday activities, have all the participants work on the same activity and then share their creations when completed.

◆ Give each parent/caregiver and child pair a pizza cardboard round, and have each pair make it into something creative. They could then write a short story together about their creation and read it to the group.

◆ Write the six basic food groups in the shape of the Food Guide Pyramid (produced by the U.S. Department of Agriculture) on a chalkboard, or white board, or on an overhead transparency. Give all the participants the same grocery store advertisement flier, and have the pairs construct a poster of a nutritious, favorite meal using the food groups. The cost of the meal could be computed on the poster. The participants could then share their meal costs and posters, and a nutritious food prize (such as a bag of popcorn) could be given to the parent/caregiver/child pair who prepared the most nutritious meal.

◆ Give each pair a large piece of construction paper and supply poster or finger paints, magic markers, colored pencils, crayons, etc. Have each pair create and write a story and illustrate it on the construction paper. Have them title their creations, and then share their stories and illustrations with the group. Later make a big "book" of the stories and illustrations that each pair created for the children to review at the next workshop session, if appropriate.

◆ Write two words on a chalkboard, white board, or on an overhead transparency. Have each pair create a two-line rhyme or a rhyming poem for each word. Have them write them down and then share these with the group.

◆ Read a short story to the whole group. Have two or more pairs work together to dramatize the story. Provide ten to 15 minutes for them to create their dramatization and to practice. Then have them share their dramatization with the group.

- Create a "monster" (as a puppet, on a poster, etc.), and write a story about the monster. Show the monster to the group and read your story about it to them.

- Ask the participants to imagine how they would feel and what they would need to do if they arrived in a new country where they were going to live forever. Have each pair write a story together about this experience and then share it with the group.

- Give all the participants the same discount store advertisement flier. Ask each pair to choose an item they would like to "buy." They should write down all the characteristics of their item—color, shape, size, etc. Then have each pair present the characteristics while the rest of the group tries to guess what the pair wants to buy. The pair should continue giving clues until the group guess the correct item.

- Ask each pair to bring their favorite game to the workshop. Have each pair show their game to the group and explain how to play the game. Have all the pairs temporarily exchange games so everyone can play a new game. Two or more pairs can play together if a game allows for that.

- Have each pair make two brown lunch sack puppets. Provide felt pieces, scraps of material, ribbon, lace, buttons, magic markers, crayons, etc. After the puppets are made, have each pair write a play and then share their puppet show with the group.

- Create a story with a one-line starter. Ask each participant to add another line until the story is complete.

◆ Provide a shoe box, scraps of construction paper, spools, pipe cleaners, etc., to each pair, and have them create something with their box. They could then write a story about their creation. Have them show their creations and read their stories to the group.

◆ Invite someone in your community who is a good story teller, or who loves to read stories or poetry, to read or tell her/his favorite story to the group. (Another idea is to invite a Brownie or Girl Scout who would like to earn her "story telling" badge. Or invite a senior citizen to tell stories from his/her youth.)

◆ Invite someone in your community who writes articles for or edits a local newspaper to speak about the purpose of a newspaper, as well as the parts of the newspaper or the articles that children may enjoy.

Reproducible Masters

Following are reproducible master copies of all the "Parent/Caregiver Handouts" referenced in the workshop presentation outline. Remember that these can also be prepared as overhead transparency masters if you wish.

Goals of This Program

For You . . .

- ◆ Enjoy reading with your child.

- ◆ Develop in your child an enjoyment of and love for reading.

- ◆ Develop your child's imagination and creativity through family reading.

- ◆ Enhance your child's learning opportunities through family reading.

- ◆ Identify or develop a suitable family reading environment.

- ◆ Implement and/or create activities that develop your child's interest in reading.

- ◆ Develop an awareness in your child that reading and writing are connected.

For Your Child . . .

- ◆ Gain a love for reading, and the motivation to learn to read.

- ◆ Talk about and enjoy the books and other materials you read together at home.

- ◆ Talk about and enjoy your reading with her/him.

- ◆ Check out more books from the school, classroom, or public library.

- ◆ Listen to his/her teacher read stories, poems, and books with greater interest.

- ◆ Talk about and bring reading "artifacts" to school, such as letters, art work, poems, and stories that were created at home.

- ◆ Ask questions and make comments more often about what is read in the classroom, at daycare, or at home.

- ◆ Understand that there is a connection between reading and writing.

Some Developmental Foundations of Literacy

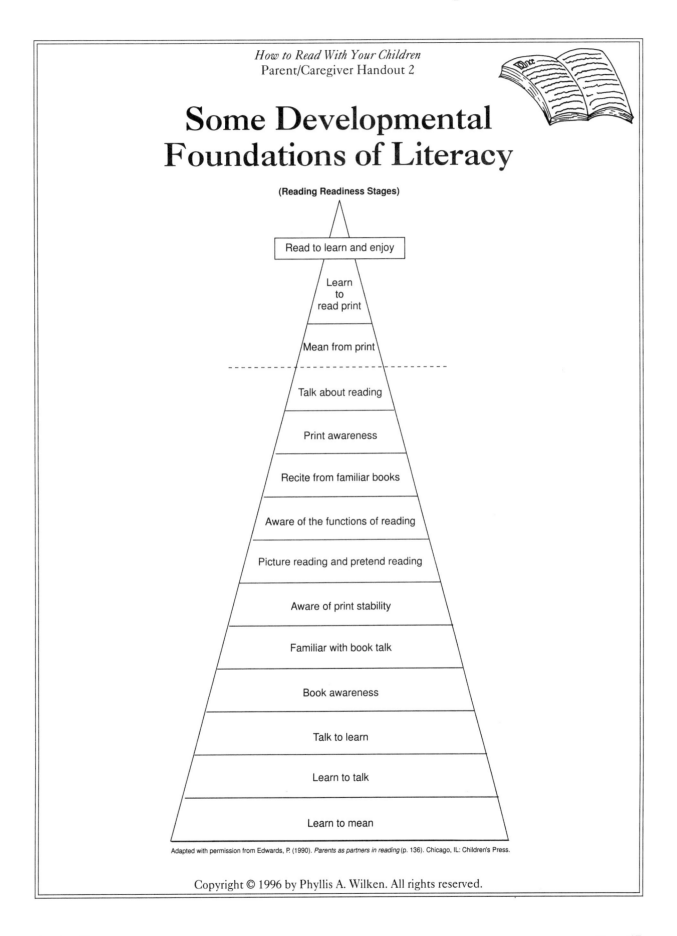

(Reading Readiness Stages)

Read to learn and enjoy

Learn to read print

Mean from print

- -

Talk about reading

Print awareness

Recite from familiar books

Aware of the functions of reading

Picture reading and pretend reading

Aware of print stability

Familiar with book talk

Book awareness

Talk to learn

Learn to talk

Learn to mean

Adapted with permission from Edwards, P. (1990). *Parents as partners in reading* (p. 136). Chicago, IL: Children's Press.

How to Read With Your Children
Parent/Caregiver Handout 3

What to Do at Home to Prepare Your Child for School

◆ Talk with your child starting at birth. Expect your child to respond, and later to talk to you by answering your questions and by asking you questions.

◆ Hug, cuddle, praise, and love your child.

◆ Help your child to learn by . . .

1. _____
2. _____
3. _____
4. _____
5. _____
6. _____
7. _____
8. _____
9. _____
10. _____
11. _____
12. _____
13. _____
14. _____
15. _____
16. _____
17. _____
18. _____
19. _____
20. _____

How to Read With Your Children
Parent/Caregiver Handout 4

What Your Child Can Learn From Reading With You

- Pictures on the book cover tell what the book is about.

- Books have a front and back cover.

- Pages should be turned one at a time.

- Print is read from top to bottom.

- Print is read from left to right.

- Print has meaning. It says something.

- Spaces are used to separate words.

- A book or story has a beginning, a middle, and an ending.

- Your child can predict what will happen in a story by looking at some of the pictures in the book.

- Books are written by a person called an author. The pictures are created by a person called an illustrator.

- Your child can learn new words and what they mean through reading.

- Your child can learn about new places and things, and many people and animals from all over the world through reading. Your child can get new ideas about how to do things or where to go to learn more about her/his ideas.

- Reading causes your child to think and to ask questions.

- Reading together is important even after your child can read on his/her own.

- Reading is a way to learn **all** of your child's life.

- Your child should realize just how much you enjoy reading with her/him. Tell your child that reading with her/him is fun!

How to Read With Your Children
Parent/Caregiver Handout 5

More Fun Positive Comments That Can Be Made!

A _____

B _____

C _____

D _____

E _____

F _____

G _____

H _____

I _____

J _____

K _____

L _____

M _____

N _____

O _____

P _____

Q _____

R _____

S _____

T _____

U _____

V _____

W _____

X _____

Y _____

Z _____

How to Read With Your Children
Parent/Caregiver Handout 6

Flash Card Masters

How to Read With Your Children
Parent/Caregiver Handout 6 (continued)

Flash Card Masters

Program Procedures

♦ Read to your child for ten minutes daily, five days per week.

♦ If you have more than one child, try to read to each child individually as much as possible.

♦ Keep a record of each child's reading times.

♦ Enjoy this special time, and let your child know that you do!

♦ Notice your child's improving reading performance.

- -

Family Reading Contact

_____

_____

Family Reading Contact

_____

_____

Family Reading Contact

_____

_____

Section Three

Publicity Packet for the Implementation of Workshop(s)

Publicity and Evaluation Suggestions

Following are three forms that can be customized for your workshop presentation(s), provided for your convenience. First is a workshop announcement, with an accompanying registration form. Information can be sent home with children from a school or daycare center, and/or it can be posted in locations such as grocery stores, libraries, churches, and school offices/libraries, in a school newsletter, etc. Next is an evaluation form, which may be helpful to you in planning future presentations and in making them more meaningful to those attending.

How to Read With Your Children

Announcement of Reading Workshop for Parents/Caregivers

Have you ever wondered what you could do to help your child with reading or with learning to read? A very important family activity is reading aloud with your children. This is an activity that will teach your child valuable academic skills, and provide a positive family experience for you both.

On _____ ,
(date[s])

_____
(name/position)

will conduct a parent/caregiver workshop(s) on reading with children at _____

_____
(location)

from _____ .
(times)

_____ will address the importance of reading aloud
(name)

to children, ways to promote reading and readiness to read at home, helpful techniques for reading aloud, questions to ask while reading, reading strategies children use, suggestions for finding and evaluating books to read, activities that use alternative reading materials, and how to connect reading and writing for children.

The workshop(s) is/are open and free to all parents and anyone else who has an interest in and an opportunity to interact and read with young children (preschool through grade 3).

Each workshop participant:
- ◯ Will receive free one copy of the *Parent/Caregiver's Guide* to the handy reference *How to Read With Your Children*.

   or
- ◯ Will need to purchase one copy of the *Parent/Caregiver's Guide* to the handy reference *How to Read With Your Children* at the cost of $_____ .

Babysitting services:
- ◯ Will not be provided.
- ◯ Will not be provided, but your children are invited to participate in the workshop.
- ◯ Will be provided at the workshop location for the minimal cost of $_____/child.

If you would like to attend, please complete and send a Registration Form to:

_____
(name/address)

or call _____ by _____ .
(telephone number)   *(date)*

We look forward to seeing you there!

(**Note:** The workshop leader named above [and possibly other workshop leaders] is available to conduct additional parent/caregiver workshops during the school year. Schools, daycare centers, preschools, churches, etc. interested in sponsoring their own workshop should contact the workshop leader.)

How to Read With Your Children

Parent/Caregiver Registration Form

Who: Parents/caregivers of preschool through grade 3 children, and others interested in reading with young children

What: *How to Read With Your Children* Workshop(s)

Where: _____

_____

Date(s): _____

_____

Time(s): _____

_____

Presented/Sponsored by: _____

_____

Costs(s) (if any): _____

_____

Participation of Children: _____

_____

Workshop(s) limited to 20 people. If more register, an additional workshop will be scheduled for

_____

(**Note:** The workshop leader named above [and possibly other workshop leaders] is available to conduct additional parent/caregiver workshops during the school year. Schools, daycare centers, preschools, churches, etc. interested in sponsoring their own workshop should contact the workshop leader.)

- -

○ Yes, I wish to attend the *How to Read With Your Children* Workshop(s) for parents/caregivers on
_____ .

Name _____

Address _____

Phone (day) _____ (evening) _____

○ I wish to use the babysitting services during the workshop(s).
The age(s) of my child(ren) is/are: _____   _____   _____

or

○ I will bring my child(ren), as invited above.
The age(s) of my child(ren) who will attend is/are: _____   _____   _____

I understand that a copy of the *Parent/Caregiver's Guide* to the book *How to Read With Your Children* will be required for the workshop(s), and will be available there.

Please return this form to _____
(name/address)

_____

by _____ , or call _____ to register.
(date)   (telephone number)

How to Read With Your Children

Evaluation Form

Please think about the workshop presentation(s) and circle the number which best describes your answer to each question.

		Strongly Agree	Agree	Neutral	Disagree	Strongly Disagree
1.	I learned that reading with my child is important for many reasons.	1	2	3	4	5
2.	I learned what to do when I read with my child.	1	2	3	4	5
3.	I learned who I should ask to help me choose books for my child.	1	2	3	4	5
4.	I learned that I am my child's first and most influential teacher.	1	2	3	4	5
5.	I learned that I should, and I will, try to read with my child for ten or more minutes per day five days per week.	1	2	3	4	5
6.	I learned what to do with my child that will help her/him to learn to read when we do not have books to read.	1	2	3	4	5

7. What was the most helpful thing you learned? _____

_____

_____

8. What else would you have liked to learn? _____

_____

_____

9. Would you recommend this workshop to another parent/caregiver? ❏ Yes ❏ No

10. Other comments _____

_____

_____

References

Barbour, J.A. (1995). The outcomes of a teacher training workshop on parent education focusing on reading with children (Doctoral dissertation, University of Illinois).

Burket, L.I. (1981). *Positive parental involvement in the area of reading during preschool years and primary grades.* (ERIC Document Reproduction Service No. ED 216 324)

Chomsky, C. (1972). Stages in language development and reading exposure. *Harvard Educational Review, 42,* 1-33.

Clark, M.M. (1976). *Young fluent readers.* London: Heinemann Educational Books.

Darabi, T.M. (1979). *Effects of a program of father-child and mother-child reading on children's reading readiness.* Gainesville, FL: University of Florida.

Durkin, D. (1966). *Children who read early.* New York: Teachers College Press.

Durkin, D. (1974). A six-year study of children who learned to read in school at the age of four. *Reading Research Quarterly, 10,* 9-61.

Durkin, D. (1978). *Teaching young children to read* (2nd ed.). Boston: Allyn and Bacon.

Edwards, P.A. (1990). *Parents as partners in reading.* Chicago: Children's Press.

Feitelson, D., Kita, B., & Goldstein, Z. (1986). Effects of listening to stories on first graders' comprehension and use of language. *Research in the Teaching of English, 20,* 339-356.

Freeman, E.B. & Wasserman, V. (1987). A will before there's a way: Preschoolers and books. *Reading Horizons, 27,* 112-122.

Harkness, F. (1981). Reading to children as a reading readiness activity. *Viewpoints in Teaching and Learning, 57,* 39-48.

Huey, E.B. (1908). *The psychology and pedagogy of reading.* New York: Macmillan.

Kelly, D. & Hellmich, N. (1996, August 21). Many parents don't read to their children. *USA Today.*

Mason, J.M., Peterman, C.L., & Kerr, B.M. (1989). *Fostering comprehension by reading books to kindergarten children* (Tech. Rep.). Urbana-Champaign: University of Illinois, Center for the Study of Reading.

McCormick, S. (1983). Reading aloud to preschoolers age 3-6: A review of the research. *Reading Horizons, 24,* 7-11.

Strickland, D.S. & Morrow, L.M. (Eds.). (1989). *Emerging literacy: Young children learn to read and write.* Newark, NJ: International Reading Association.

Teale, W.H. (1978). Positive environments for learning to read: What studies of early readers tell us. *Language Arts, 55,* 922-932.

Toomey, D.M. (1986). *How parental participation and involvement in schools can increase educational inequality.* Melbourne: A.A.R.E. Conference paper.

Wilken, P.A. (1990). *A survey of Chapter 1 teachers: A summary* (Tech. Rep.). Urbana-Champaign: Univrsity of Illinois, Center for the Study of Reading.

Wilken, P.A. (1992). *Teachers' views of Chapter 1 programs* (Tech. Rep.). Urbana-Champaign: University of Illinois, Center for the Study of Reading.

Other Publications by the Author

■■■ How to Read With Your Children: Parent/Caregiver's Guide

Reading is a skill that opens doors for life. It is also a skill that improves with practice. In *How to Read With Your Children*, the former director of the nationally recognized Garden Hills Reading Program shares simple suggestions about why, what, where, when, and how parents and other caregivers can read to preschool and primary grade children.

This inviting handbook lists hundreds of ideas that parents/caregivers can use as reading partners in daily ten-minute read-aloud sessions with their children. Included are suggestions on selecting appropriate books, what to do when you do not have books to read, positive comments that can be made, and ways to help children make the reading/writing connection.

Parents/caregivers who read with their children on a regular basis have the opportunity to demonstrate the importance of reading, observe their children's reading development and performance, and fully participate in making their children lifelong, independent readers.

■■■ Turning Our School Around: Seven Commonsense Steps to School Improvement

Would you like to know how a troubled school with many special needs students turned around, and in five years received the U.S. Department of Education Blue Ribbon Award for Excellence in Elementary Education? Learn how this elementary school, using common sense programs, enabled children from a diverse, multicultural, transient community to raise their reading and math scores at each grade level by three to four months in three years. Learn how the parents helped to maintain this gain by reading for 6,000 hours at home with the help of the nationally recognized Garden Hills Family Reading Club. Learn how 91-98% of the students earned "Garden Hills Number One" student recognition for exemplary behavior over a five-year period. This exciting story was written by the school's former principal, Phyllis A. Wilken.

Order Form

Sopris West

Product Code	Product Title	Qty.	Unit Price*	Total Price
85SET	How to Read With Your Children Set (5 Parent/Caregiver's Guide and 1 Educator/Leader's Guide)		$35.00	
85PG	How to Read With Your Children: Parent/Caregiver's Guide (individual copy)		$ 9.00	
85EG	How to Read With Your Children: Educator/Leader's Guide (individual copy)		$ 9.00	
85PGSET	How to Read With Your Children: Parent/Caregiver's Guide (5 copies)		$29.00	
96TURN	Turning Our School Around		$15.50	
—	Sopris West Catalog		FREE	
			Subtotal	
			Shipping/Handling**	
			Sales Tax (CO residents add 3%.)	
			Total Amount Due	

*Prices subject to change without notice.
**10% of total price, $4 minimum

Bill to _____

_____

_____

Phone ( ) _____

Ship to (if different) _____

_____

_____

Phone ( ) _____

Four Easy Ways to Order

FAX
303.776.5934

Phone Toll Free
800.547.6747

Mail to Sopris West
1140 Boston Avenue
Longmont, CO 80501

Internet
http://www.sopriswest.com

Method of Payment

❑ VISA   ❑ MasterCard   ❑ Purchase Order (Attach copy.)   ❑ Check/Money Order (Make payable to Sopris West.)

Account Number   Expiration Date

Print name of cardholder.   Cardholder sign here.